Dweeb-A-Mania

Sarah Middleton

methuen | drama

LONDON • NEW YORK • OXFORD • NEW DELHI • SYDNEY

METHUEN DRAMA
Bloomsbury Publishing Plc, 50 Bedford Square, London, WC1B 3DP, UK
Bloomsbury Publishing Inc, 1359 Broadway, New York, NY 10018, USA
Bloomsbury Publishing Ireland, 29 Earlsfort Terrace, Dublin 2,
D02 AY28, Ireland

BLOOMSBURY, METHUEN DRAMA and the Methuen
Drama logo are trademarks of Bloomsbury Publishing Plc.

First published in Great Britain 2025

Copyright © Sarah Middleton, 2025

Sarah Middleton has asserted their right under the Copyright, Designs
and Patents Act, 1988, to be identified as Author of this work.

Cover artwork photography by Christa Holka, design by Anna Fernandez

Cover Cast: Clare Beresford and Lakeisha Lynch-Stevens

All rights reserved. No part of this publication may be: i) reproduced or
transmitted in any form, electronic or mechanical, including photocopying,
recording or by means of any information storage or retrieval system without
prior permission in writing from the publishers; or ii) used or reproduced in
any way for the training, development or operation of artificial intelligence (AI)
technologies, including generative AI technologies. The rights holders
expressly reserve this publication from the text and data mining exception as
per Article 4(3) of the Digital Single Market Directive (EU) 2019/790.

Bloomsbury Publishing Plc does not have any control over, or responsibility
for, any third-party websites referred to or in this book. All internet addresses
given in this book were correct at the time of going to press. The author and
publisher regret any inconvenience caused if addresses have changed or sites
have ceased to exist, but can accept no responsibility for any such changes.

No rights in incidental music or songs contained in the work are hereby
granted and performance rights for any performance/presentation
whatsoever must be obtained from the respective copyright owners.

All rights whatsoever in this play are strictly reserved and application
for performance etc. should be made before rehearsals begin to The
Haworth Agency, Studio 103, Babel Studios, 158b Kentish Town Road,
London, NW5 2AG (permissions@haworthagency.co.uk). No performance
may be given unless a licence has been obtained.

A catalogue record for this book is available from the British Library.

A catalog record for this book is available from the Library of Congress.

ISBN: PB: 978-1-3505-9819-5
ePDF: 978-1-3505-9820-1
eBook: 978-1-3505-9821-8

Series: Modern Plays

Typeset by Mark Heslington Ltd, Scarborough, North Yorkshire

For product safety related questions contact
productsafety@bloomsbury.com.

To find out more about our authors and books visit
www.bloomsbury.com and sign up for our newsletters.

Dweeb-A-Mania

Dweeb-A-Mania was a Polka Theatre production and the winner of the Polka Playwriting Award 2025, generously funded by The Garek Trust and supported by Cockayne and London Community Foundation. Selected by Polka Playwriting Award Judges, shortlisted in consultation with a reading panel and Polka Grads Young Readers.

It was first presented at Polka Theatre in October 2025. The cast and creative team who made the show were:

Cast

Kemi	Chidera Ikechukwu
Norah	Amy Blake
Bentley	Wesley Ruthven
Lily	Grace Carroll

Creatives

Writer	Sarah Middleton
Director	Hannah Stone
Set & Costume Designer	Katie Lias
Composer & Sound Designer	Ellie Isherwood
Lighting Designer	Jane Lalljee
Movement Director	DK Fashola
Fight Director	Nora Iso-Kungas
Production Manager	Nick Flintoff
Stage Manager	Iona Hicks
Set Construction	Mark Bramfitt & Basement 94
Scenic Artist	Fani Parali

For Polka Theatre

Artistic Director	Helen Matravers
Executive Director	Lynette Shanbury
Head of Production	Adam Crosthwaite
Head of Creative Learning	Polly Simmonds
Head of Development	Georgina Davey
Head of Sales and Marketing	Sara Hijazi Greenwood
Head of Finance	Bernadette Cava

Head of Operations and Visitor Services	Woonie Chan
Senior Producer	Kate Bradshaw
Technical Manager	Peter Hatherall
Wardrobe Manager	Annie James
Deputy Technical Manager	Jerry Parsons
Associate Director	Roman Stefanski
Assistant Producer	Abigayle Bartley
Birkbeck Resident Assistant Director	Peter O'Connor-Smart
Community Engagement Manager	Chusi Amoros
Participation Manager (Maternity Cover)	Jemima Deboo-Sands
Schools Manager	Lizzie Corscaden
Community Officer (Maternity Cover)	Lucie Long
Marketing Manager	Julia Canavan
Marketing Officer	Victoria Dowding
Marketing Assistant	Mia Sinclair
Sales and Ticketing Manger	Laura Perry
Sales and Ticketing Supervisors	Alexander Benjamin
	Sara Al Ghanem
Development and Events Manager	Jemima Unsworth
Trusts Relationship Manager	Lizzie Lord
Development Assistant	Rosa Montague-Vaughan
Senior Finance Officer	Gloria Mason
Finance Assistant	Rosie Simmonds
Visitor Services Manager	Ruth Cowell
Volunteer Coordinator	Emma Harvey
Buildings and Operations Manager	Louis Forte
Commercial and Hires Officer	Ross Bonny
Café Manager	Bruno Fawzi Izem
Café Supervisor	Dora Chan

With huge thanks to the practitioners, facilitators and volunteers who work so hard at Polka to make sure we empower and inspire children daily.

Chidera Ikechukwu – Kemi

Chidera is a 2025 graduate of Arts Ed. Her credits whilst training included: Shireen in *Now You Know,* Nurse in *Romeo and Juliet,* Flo in *Picnic*, Claire in Proof and Maria in *Uncle Vanya*. Screen credits include: *Waterloo Road* (BBC) and *Lagging* (CBBC).

Amy Blake – Norah

Amy is a Yorkshire actor, powered by tea and vegetables. Young audiences might recognise her from *The Stolen Stories of Winterlight* and *The Storymaker's Apprentice* with Libellule Theatre, *New Girl* with Thunk-it Theatre or for chasing after a dinosaur with *Jurassic Earth*. Grown-ups may have seen Amy in Sky TV's most successful comedy *Brassic* and BBC's *Casualty.*

Wesley Ruthven – Bentley

Wesley trained at LAMDA and his credits whilst training included: Sean in *Scuttlers*, Angelo in *Measure for Measure,* Tuzenbach *in Three Sisters,* John Buchanan Jr. in *Summer and Smoke*, Chris Gilfoy in *Chequered Flags to Chequered Futures*, Harry in *Graham: The World's Fastest Blind Runner* and *Petruchio* in *The Taming of the Shrew.*

Screen credits include T in *Anonymous (*Thirtyone2526 Limited, supported by Amazon Video) and Fraser in *Blurred Lines* (LAMDA).

Workshops include *The Arsonist* for National Theatre Studio and *Moral Animal* and *Generational Class Play* for Orange Tree Theatre.

Grace Carroll – Lily

Dweeb-A-Mania is Grace's professional debut. She graduated from Arts Ed in 2024, where her credits included Amy in *Breathing Corpses* and Nell in *Nell Gwynn*.

Sarah Middleton – Writer

Sarah is an award-winning writer from Derby. Her first play *Shewolves* toured the UK before transferring to Southwark Playhouse in 2023, and is published by Concord Theatricals/Samuel French. Musicals include *Pinocchio* and *Little Red Riding Hood* (Nottingham Playhouse), *The Wishing Stone* (Separate Doors/Derby Theatre/Chichester Festival Theatre) and *Wilf Goes Wild* (MPTheatricals). Projects in development include *Vamp*, a gig musical about an all-female, all-vampire rock band.

With director Hannah Stone, Sarah co-runs Shewolves Productions – a Midlands-based company telling stories about women who stray from the path.

Sarah is the recipient of a Hosking Houses residency, a Peggy Ramsay grant and a National Theatre Peter Shaffer commission.

Hannah Stone – Director

Hannah (she/her) is a director and theatre maker. Credits as director include: R&D *Vamp* for Shewolves Productions (2025); R&D *The King Stone* by Charlotte East at National Theatre Studio (2025); *The Trials* at Nottingham Playhouse (2024); *Ruby's Worry* for Mishmash Theatre (2024); R&D *The Mother and Son Play* by Joshua Parr at Young Vic (2023); *Shewolves* by Sarah Middleton, national tour and run at Southwark Playhouse (2023); *Goldilocks and the Three Bears* by Anna Wheatley at Nottingham Playhouse (2022); *Aidy the Awesome* for Rebel Sparks national tour, commissioned by Curve Theatre, Leicester (2022); and *Pinocchio* for Nottingham Playhouse and Mercury Theatre (2019/22).

Hannah co-runs Rebel Sparks and Shewolves Productions. She was the 2024 RTST Sir Peter Hall Director's Award runner-up and was an Associate Artist at Nottingham Playhouse in 2021–23.

Katie Lias – Set & Costume Designer

Katie trained at RADA and was a resident trainee designer with the RSC.

Katie won the Pantomime Award for Best Costume Design 2025 and was also nominated for Best Set Design. She has additionally been nominated for three Broadway World Awards for Best Set Design.

Recent work includes: *Burnt at the Stake* (Globe Theatre); *Handbagged* (National Theatre & Queen's Theatre Hornchurch UK tour), *Bleak Expectations* (Criterion Theatre); *Jack and the Beanstalk, Sleeping Beauty* (Salisbury Playhouse); *The Importance of Being Earnest* (Mercury Theatre, Colchester); *The Two Popes, The Wasp* (English Theatre Frankfurt); *To Wong Foo The Musical* (Hope Mill Theatre); *Notes from a Small Island, Spike, As You Like It, Just So, Hamlet, The Prince and the Pauper, Journey's End* (Watermill Theatre); *A Midsummer Night's Dream, Macbeth, Twelfth Night, Romeo and Juliet* (UK tour and Wilton's Music Hall); *Lady Chatterley's Lover* (UK tour); *The Strange Case of Dr Jekyll and Mr Hyde* (Storyhouse Theatre); *Eclipse* (Lyric Hammersmith); *Cinderella, Dick Whittington and His Cat* (Costume Designer, Lyric Hammersmith); *Grandad, Me and Teddy Too, Alice in Wonderland, Shake, Rattle and Roll, My Brother My Sister and Me* (Polka Theatre); *Address Unknown* (Soho Theatre); *The Tempest, Shakespeare in a Suitcase* (RSC tour)

Ellie Isherwood – Composer & Sound Designer

Ellie is a sound designer, composer, actor/musician and synth-pop artist (BYFYN). Her 'quietly ground-breaking' work spans a vast array of forms, from site-specific theatre to binaural audio experiences. Recent work includes composition for the stage adaptation of Lemony Snicket's *The Dark*.

Jane Lalljee – Lighting Designer

Upcoming projects include *Mother Goose* (Mercury Theatre, Colchester). Recent projects include: *Noises Off* (Stephen Joseph Theatre); *Love's Labour's Lost (sort of)* (Stephen Joseph Theatre/Shakespeare North Playhouse); *Tidy* (Theatr Iolo & Polka Theatre); *Nutcracker* (Wales Millennium Centre); *Pinocchio* (Taunton Brewhouse); *Aladdin* (Theatre Royal, Bury St Edmunds); *Little Women* (York Theatre Royal); *Dracula, The Bloody Truth* (SJT/Bolton Octagon); *Parti Priodas* (Theatr Cymru Welsh tour); *The House with Chicken Legs* (Les Enfants Terribles national tour); *Jeeves and Wooster* (Salisbury Playhouse/Bolton Octagon); *Now and Then* (English Theatre, Frankfurt); *The Card* (New Vic Theatre, Newcastle-under-Lyme); *Rose* (Ambassador Theatre)

DK Fashola – Movement Director

dkfash is an interdisciplinary artist working across stage, film and entertainment. As writer and director work includes: *Is Dat U Yh?* (Brixton House); *by their fruits & Fragments of a Complicated Mind* (Theatre503); *Scalped* (Without Walls national tour). Movement includes: National Theatre, Royal Shakespeare Company, Bush Theatre, Royal Exchange Theatre, Unicorn Theatre and Sheffield Theatres.

A range of other work includes the UK premiere of *Bootycandy* (Gate Theatre), choreography for *Wizkid* (Zinarts), twerk artist for bounce legend Big Freedia and 24 Studio Wayne McGregor – Resident 6 Artist.

She is the founder of Initiative.dkf, recipient of the 21 Eclipse Award.

Nora Iso-Kungas – Fight Director

Nora is a fight director working in theatre, TV and film. Having trained as an actor and fight performer in East 15 acting and fight performance course she combines her acting background with fight and martial arts training to create action that is specific to the storyline, uniquely designed for each performer and captivating for the audience.

Nick Flintoff – Production Manager

Nick trained at RADA and studied documentary film at the MetFilm School. He currently works as a theatre production manager and filmmaker. He worked all over the world for Imagination Ltd and later worked at the National Theatre for ten years in their New Work Department as the Technical Associate, developing new work for the main stages and other national theatres. More recently he went on to be the Production Manager for the Watermill Theatre in Newbury, where he worked on the award-winning musical revival of *The Lord of the Rings*.

Iona Hicks – Stage Manager

Iona graduated from Bristol Old Vic Theatre School in July 2024 where she specialised in stage management. Since then, she has worked as the stage manager on book for multiple productions including: *Playfight* tour (Grace Dickson Productions); *Boxville* (Cardboard Adventures); *The Snowy Day* (Can't Sit Still) and *Let's Build* (Polka Theatre). She has also enjoyed being the Deputy Stage Manager/Show Caller for the launch event of Soho Theatre Walthamstow and continues to love her work in stage management.

ABOUT POLKA THEATRE

Polka is one of just a handful of dedicated children's venues in the UK. It underwent a major renovation, re-opening as a state-of-the-art hub for families, schools and the community in 2021. Polka presents a year-round programme of new work, visiting shows, and Creative Learning activities for 0–12-year-olds. They continue to pioneer developments in children's theatre, nurture artistic talent in the sector, and maintain an international reputation while serving local communities. Children are involved at every stage of the creative process and lead the way in Early Years Theatre. Creative Learning is central to Polka's mission – with shows supported by tailored community and school initiatives. In 2024 Polka Theatre was named the *UK's Most Welcoming Theatre* at the UK Theatre Awards, Merton Borough's *Best Business*, and Time and Leisure's *Family Attraction of the Year*.

Polka Theatre is a Charity and is grateful for the continued support of Arts Council England and the many charitable trusts, business partners and individuals that continue to support the vital work of the theatre.

ABOUT THE GAREK TRUST

The Garek Trust is a newly established charitable trust based in London. Their goal is to give access and exposure to the Performing Arts to underprivileged children and young people through a variety of means.

ABOUT COCKAYNE AND LONDON COMMUNITY FOUNDATION

Cockayne is a private arts foundation based in San Francisco. It supports diverse and ground-breaking arts projects in the performing, literary and visual arts in London through a donor advised programme, 'Cockayne Grants for the Arts', held at the London Community Foundation.

Writer's Note

My Uncle sometimes comes to stay when he's working in London. On his suitcase is a massive neon yellow sticker reading 'NERD'. He's proud of being brainy, which I think is awesome. When you're an adult, it's no big deal if you read the Encyclopedia Brittanica for fun, or spend your weekend watching documentaries about space. But when you're eleven, it can feel a bit different.

The alternative (but less exciting) title for this play would be 'The Last Days of Year Six'. The end of Primary School is a pivotal, transitional time. I wanted to write a play about this chapter of childhood – when everything is changing and you're torn between being true to yourself and being part of the group. This play explores the painful realisation that other people might not care about the things that matter to you, and – even worse – might laugh at your enthusiasm. But I hope it's also funny, sparky and uplifting, and reminds us all that girls can do anything – including wrestling.

So, this one goes out to the bookish, nerdy kids who feel like outsiders just because they like learning. Find the other dweebs. Band together. And let's all get stickers :)

Acknowledgements

Thank you to . . .

Everyone at Polka, The Garek Trust, Cokayne Foundation, The London Community Foundation and Methuen Drama for caring so much about theatre for children, and for launching this extraordinary new award.

Polka Grads and New Voices for your enthusiasm and feedback.

Hannah Stone, for asking the best questions.

Helen Arney, for making science explosively fun.

Andy, for laughing at all the funny bits.

And to my family; thank you, thank you, thank you for always celebrating dweebiness.

Dweeb-A-Mania

For Lizzie, who has dweeb power running through her veins

Characters

Kemi, *eleven*
Norah, *eleven*
Lily, *ten*
Bentley, *eleven*

Prologue

The blinding lights of a wrestling arena. Anthemic music blasts!

A whack! A slam! A roar!

The sound of a referee smacking the mat three times. A bell rings out. The crowd goes wild!

It transforms into a school bell as the crowd fades away . . .

One

A school playground.

The bell rings as two nerdy girls, **Kemi** *(eleven) and* **Norah** *(eleven) run in, reading enormous books. They bump into each other.*

Norah *smiles.* **Kemi** *doesn't.*

Lily *(a scrawny ten-year-old) runs to the middle of the playground.*

Bentley *(eleven) struts in, with his school jumper draped around his neck like a cape. He dominates the space in a majestic display of pure masculinity.*

He gives **Lily** *a signal and she stops the music.*

Bentley Announcing . . . the end of Year 6 graduation party! The biggest and best party of all time . . . Bentley's Wrestling Party! WWE style!

He strikes a killer wrestling pose.

He builds up a chant with the audience, assisted by **Lily**.

Bentley When I say Bentley, you say champ. Bentley –

Champ!

Bentley –

Champ!

Our dad's getting a wrestling ring and forty-three rotisserie chickens. And I'm gonna be the champion.

He approaches an audience member.

Show me your muscles. YES. You're invited. You can fight me. Everybody cool is invited. You, you, you, you – everybody –

He spots **Kemi** *and* **Norah**.

– except Kemi and Norah. Ok, bye.

Lily *is about to play* **Bentley**'s *exit music, when* –

Norah Wait – why aren't I invited?

Kemi Or me? Why aren't I?

He turns.

Bentley It's a party. It's for cool people.

Kemi I'm cool.

He flicks her book.

Bentley You read the dictionary at break.

Kemi And I'm a very keen wrestler.

Norah Same. Extremely keen.

Kemi *glares at them.*

Bentley What does WWE stand for?

He points to **Norah** *to test her.*

Norah Wrestling wow, exciting!

Bentley *makes an incorrect buzzer sound.*

He points to **Kemi**.

Kemi Wrestlers wrestling everywhere!

Another incorrect buzzer sound.

Bentley When September comes, we'll be in Year 7. The whole of Harris Academy will hear about my wrestling party. That I dominated in the ring. They'll know I won the champion's belt! I can't have dweebs dragging down my vibe.

Kemi Dweebs?

Bentley Yeah. Dweebs.

(*To* **Lily**.) Sis! Exit music!

Bentley *struts off.*

Sis!

Lily *runs off after him.*

Kemi *immediately opens her dictionary and looks something up.*

Norah Dweeb? What even is a dweeb?

Kemi *finds the definition. She reads it.*

Kemi Do excuse me.

Norah What does it say? What's a dweeb?

Kemi *slams the dictionary shut and trots off.*

Norah Kemi! Wait! What's a dweeb?!

Norah *runs after her.*

Two

The old sports hall.

Kemi *has commandeered an iPad.* **Norah** *catches up with her.*

Kemi Stop following me!

Norah *looks around.*

Norah We used to do apparatus in here in Year 3. Do you remember? And after school club. They keep the arts and craft stuff in here –

Kemi Shush! I need to concentrate.

Norah Why are we in here?

Kemi It's quiet. Nobody comes here. It's good for concentrating.

Norah *watches over* **Kemi***'s shoulder.* **Kemi** *tries to move away from* **Norah**.

Norah 'What is the definition of "dweeb"?' Good idea!

Kemi It's bad form to read over someone's shoulder.

Norah What does it say? I'm a dweeb too, apparently. I have a right to know. What are we?!

Kemi 'Dweeb: a person who is boring, studious or socially inept.'

Pause.

Norah How utterly mortifying! I can't have this. I can't go into Year 7 with the whole of Harris Academy thinking I'm a dweeb! Oh my goodness! They're going to whisper 'dweeb' at me in the corridors. They're going to leave Post-It notes on my locker with 'dweeb' scrawled in gel pen. They're going to flush my head down the toilet whilst chanting 'dweeb, dweeb, dweeb' –

Kemi Please be quiet. I'm trying to problem-solve.

Norah *reads over* **Kemi***'s shoulder again as she types.*

Kemi 'What is the opposite of a dweeb?'

She hits search.

'A champion.'

She types again:

'Champion wrestlers. Professional wrestlers.'

She scans the results.

World Wrestling Entertainment.

Kemi/Norah WWE!

Norah Wow. Look at them. So powerful.

Kemi So shiny.

Norah So muscular.

Kemi So utterly un-dweeby . . . I'm going to become a pro wrestler.

Norah So am I.

Kemi Stop copying me, stop stealing my ideas!

Norah It's not stealing, we're going to do it together.

Kemi *folds her arms.*

Norah You can't fly across the ring on your own. You can't bodyslam thin air. But if we work together – if we join forces, we can do it. We can become pro wrestlers.

Kemi *still isn't sold.* **Norah** *scrolls through more images.*

Norah There's a winner. There's a champion's belt.

She shows **Kemi** *a photo of a pro wrestler lifting a shiny metal belt.*

Norah Year Seven is the start of the rest of our lives. It matters. If we sneak in to Bentley's party and present an undeniable routine of wrestling excellence, everyone will see. We'll lay the foundations for the rest of our lives. Not as a dweebs, but as heroes.

Come on, Kemi.

Kemi . . . Ok.

Norah Yes! Meet in here after lunch. Wear your PE kit.

Three

Lunchtime. The old sports hall.

Kemi *and* **Norah** *run in, wearing their PE kits. They put down their huge, dorky backpacks.*

Norah Everyone's talking about Bentley's graduation party. Molly-May cried because it clashes with her ballet exam, Gracie's abandoning veganism to try a rotisserie chicken, and Alfie's planning to steal his grandma's credit card and order two hundred temporary tattoos of Bentley's face!

Kemi Breathe.

Norah This party is fast becoming a life and death situation.

Kemi How do you know all this?

Norah I eat lunch on my own and I listen.

Kemi *whips out a small, stapled booklet.*

Norah What's that?

Kemi A training plan. For my – for our – wrestling project.

Norah Let me see. When did you make this?

Kemi At break. I stayed inside and consulted the internet.

Norah How resourceful.

Kemi Indeed.

She flicks through the booklet.

Phase one: individual strength training and cardio workouts.

Norah What about kicking and punching? We need to make it look like we're having a fight. A real, bloodthirsty wrestle-to-the-death! That's what WWE is! Squashing each other, slamming each other's heads into the mat. It has to be brutal. Barbaric. Gladiatorial!

Kemi I'd like to start with a gentle warm-up.

Norah Wait!

She runs to her bag and pulls a sign out of it.

Nearly forgot.

She holds it up.

Kemi (*reading the sign*)   'Extremely Serious Homework Club for Nerdy Science Kids'.

Norah *sticks it to the door.*

Norah   Now nobody will disturb us.

Kemi   How sneaky of you.

Norah   I'll stick it on the door.

She flourishes the sign, and –

Owch! Papercut –

Kemi *turns away and stops breathing for a second.*

Kemi   Are you bleeding?

Norah   No. Sign!

Norah *sticks the sign on the door.*

Let's start.

Kemi   Shoulder press walking lunge. Ten. Go!

They begin walking lunges with shoulder presses.

Norah   I'm so unfit.

Kemi   NEXT!

She runs to her rucksack and pulls out several enormous books.

Norah   Encyclopedia Britannica!

Kemi   From the library. Dense.

She hands one to **Norah**.

Kemi   Weighted squats.

They begin squatting, each holding a volume of Encyclopedia Britannica.

When we're in Year 7, there'll be a plethora of parties. Probably, like, every single weekend. Do you think we'll get invited? Once we've proved our awesomeness?

Kemi The probability is high.

Norah And sleepovers. We'll have sleepovers all the time.

Kemi Guaranteed.

Norah We haven't had a sleepover for ages. Not since –

Pause.

Kemi I have.

Norah Have you?! When?

Kemi I went to Space Camp.

Norah Space Camp?!

Kemi In the Easter holidays. I camped out at Greenwich Observatory.

Norah I didn't know that!

Kemi I'm a girl of many mysteries. Star jumps. Fifty.

Norah Fifty?!

They drop the books and begin star jumps.

My aerobic fitness is way below par.

Kemi We need to distract our brains.

Norah With what?

Kemi I have just the thing. New vocabulary for Harris Academy.

Norah We need to learn new vocabulary?

Kemi Obviously. We're reinventing ourselves!

Norah Like Doctor Who.

Kemi At Harris Academy, I'm not going to say 'yes', I'm going to say 'hundy-p'.

Norah Hundy-what?

Kemi 'Hundy-p'. It means a hundred per cent. But shorter and better. Cool people say it. Non-dweebs.

Norah 'Hundy-p'...

Kemi And I might describe things as 'sick'. Even if they're not vomit-inducing.

Norah 'Sick'. Right. Got it.

Kemi I think it's going to suit me, being a pro wrestler.

Norah And me. It's going to be extremely 'sick' indeed.

They flex their muscles, pose and stick their tongues out like pro wrestlers.

Norah Pro wrestlers...

Kemi Pro wrestlers!

The school bell rings. **Norah** *grabs her bag.*

See you on Monday, then –

Kemi Wait! I'd like to set a homework task for the weekend. A 'History of Wrestling' research project. I'll explore ancient Babylonian sports and the South American tradition, and you'll swot up on French cave drawings and modern Japanese wrestling.

Norah Wow. Fascinating.

Kemi And we'll continue with our workouts every day. No pain, no gain.

Norah Good plan.

Kemi Sick plan.

She grabs the booklet back.

Kemi I'd better keep hold of that. Wouldn't want it to go missing . . .

Pause.

Norah Have a good weekend.

Kemi *grabs her bag. They both leave.*

Four

Bentley's *bedroom.*

He is sitting on his bed, looking at a small plastic box.

Lily *comes in.* **Bentley** *panics, slams the box shut, hides it and pretends to be training.*

Bentley Oh my God, knock. What d'you want? I'm trying to practise, I'm trying to –

Lily This arrived.

She hands **Bentley** *a parcel. He opens it and pulls out a replica championship wrestling belt.*

Bentley The champion's belt . . .

He carefully places the belt on his bed. **Lily** *hovers nervously.*

Bentley What d'you want?!

Lily Um – ok. There's – there's this big new Year 5 science project. We all have to 'demonstrate an experiment'. On our own. In front of the whole class.

Bentley So?

Lily So I thought . . . cos you're older and, like, good at stuff, you could maybe . . . help me?

Bentley Ask Dad.

Lily He said I should do whatever ChatGPT says.

Bentley Do that, then.

Lily It says the best experiment is an 'air cannon vortex'. But I don't really get it. You might, though. You're in Year 6.

Bentley Science is for dweebs. And I've gotta train. Gotta get 'swoll'!

He jumps into a push-up position.

Nine . . . ten . . .

Lily I could show you the website. While you do your – your push-ups, or whatever?

Bentley No! This is private, it's a private gym –

Lily It's a bedroom.

Bentley It's both, actually. It's both. Go, get out. I don't have time for nerdy Year 5 stuff.

Lily Fine.

She goes to the door.

She sees something on the floor. She picks it up.

Look.

Bentley What?!

Lily It's a sequin.

Bentley It must be yours, you must have trod it in on your big feet. Bin it, just bin it.

Pause.

Get out. I need to train, I need to practise my moves, my killer moves! Take this, go!

He shoves **Lily** *towards the door and throws her the empty cardboard box.*

Lily *leaves.* **Bentley** *looks at the champion's belt.*

Five

Monday. The old sports hall.

Kemi *and* **Norah** *put elbow and knee pads on.*

Kemi In my research at the weekend, I discovered that in WWE, there are two types of wrestler: Heels and Faces. Heels are the baddies, and Faces are the goodies.

Norah Heels and Faces?!

Kemi Heel means 'a double-crosser, someone untrustworthy'. Heels always lose. Faces always win.

Kemi/Norah I'd like to be the Face.

Norah But you always win things.

Kemi No I don't.

Norah You won the Junior Chess League.

Kemi You won the maths challenge.

Norah You won the Year 5 spelling competition! You got a book token! You always win. It's my turn. I should be the Face.

Kemi Let's decide fairly.

She offers her hand to **Norah**.

Thumb war.

They embark on an extremely intense, high-stakes thumb war.

Eventually **Norah** *wins.*

Norah There. I win. Fair and square. I'm the Face, you're the Heel.

Kemi *is annoyed.*

Norah In my research, I found the perfect move for the end of our fight. It's called . . . the Atomic Drop. We start by facing each other. The Face stands here. The Heel stands there.

Norah *and* **Kemi** *face each other in wrestling stances.*

Norah You run at me. Then I lift you over my head and slam you onto the mat. Ready?

Kemi Don't slam me too hard.

Norah Go.

They have a go. **Norah** *manages to half-lift* **Kemi**, *but they get stuck.*

Kemi Is this right?!

Norah You're squashing my butt cheek!

Kemi Put me down!

Norah I'm supposed to slam you!

Lily *comes in unseen.*

If we don't commit to this, we'll fail in our secret plan to become wrestlers and crash Bentley's party!

Pause.

Lily Is this the 'Extremely Serious Homework Club for Nerdy Science Kids'?

Norah/Kemi No!/Yes?!

Pause.

Lily The – the Year 5 science project's coming up. And I – I need help.

Kemi Why would we help you? You're Bentley's sister.

Lily I heard what you said. About becoming wrestlers and crashing my brother's party. I should tell him.

Kemi No!

Norah Please!

Lily But I could forget to tell Bentley, if you help me with my science project. We could make a deal.

Norah A deal?

Kemi I don't make deals with Year 5s.

Lily Why not?

Kemi I find them to be an extremely untrustworthy year group.

Norah But she's Bentley's little sister!

Lily I have a name, actually. I want to prove to everyone that I can do stuff, that I can talk in front of the whole class and do my own experiment. I want to do an air cannon vortex!

Pause.

Norah This changes things.

Kemi We'd like to discuss this privately.

Kemi *and* **Norah** *make a huddle.*

Kemi I've got to admit, an air cannon vortex is a tempting experiment.

Norah And if we don't help her, she'll tell Bentley, and then it's game over.

They turn back to **Lily**.

Norah/Kemi We accept.

Lily Cool.

We'll help you with your science project and in return you'll keep our plan a secret –

Kemi And coach us!

Lily/Norah What?!

Kemi You know about wrestling. Bentley told everyone he watches wrestling every single night.

Norah And that you have unlimited screen time.

Lily But – I'm not a coach. I'm not good at telling people what to do.

Norah If you're going to do a science presentation in front of the whole class, we need to seriously improve your self-confidence.

Kemi I bet you already know way more about wrestling than we do.

Norah All you have to do is watch our moves and tell us what we're doing wrong –

Kemi And make sure it's safe.

Norah/Kemi Please?

Lily Ok. I'll give it a go.

She shakes their hands.

Norah Air cannon vortex; nice choice. Epic. Your neural synapses will be screaming for mercy.

Lily So will your muscles. Wrestling's well hard.

Kemi We'll meet here every day. At lunchtime, we wrestle. And at afternoon play, we science.

Norah I can get all the equipment. I know the code to the science cupboard.

Kemi Oh do you?

The bell rings for the end of lunch.

They grab their things and head to the door.

Norah See you later, Bentley's sister. Wait – what's your actual name?

Lily Lily.

Kemi Welcome to the team, Lily.

18 Dweeb-A-Mania

Six A

Wrestling music blasts as an epic, movie-style montage begins . . .

Bentley *speaks into a microphone in a wrestling announcer's voice.*

Bentley Five days to go, till the party of the century!

He gets the audience chanting 'Bentley is the champ'.

Meanwhile, in the sports hall . . .

Lily *pulls up a video on the iPad. She instructs* **Norah** *and* **Kemi** *as they attempt The Low Blow:*

Kemi *crawls over to a standing* **Norah** *and punches her pathetically in the thigh.*

They both look to **Lily**. *She gives them a thumbs down.*

Six B

Bentley *speaks into the microphone in a wrestling announcer's voice.*

Bentley Four days to go, till the party of the century!

More chanting.

He admires his muscles. Meanwhile, in the sports hall . . .

Lily *checks the coast is clear. Then,* **Norah** *and* **Kemi** *smuggle science equipment into the sports hall: lab coats, goggles, elastic bands, etc.*

Six C

Bentley *speaks into the microphone in a wrestling announcer's voice.*

Bentley Three days to go, till the party of the century!

More chanting!

Meanwhile, in the sports hall:

Lily *shows* **Kemi** *and* **Norah** *how to do 'The People's Elbow'.*

Six D

Bentley *speaks into the microphone in a wrestling announcer's voice.*

Bentley   Two days to go, till the party of the century!

More chanting. He dropkicks an imaginary opponent.

Meanwhile, in the sports hall . . .

Lily *coaches* **Norah** *and* **Kemi** *through their Finisher: The Atomic Drop.*

Kemi *swings a punch over* **Norah**'s *head.* **Norah** *intercepts it and lifts* **Kemi**. *They get completely tangled.*

Lily *points expertly at the problem.*

Seven

Bentley *speaks into the microphone in a wrestling announcer's voice.*

Bentley   One day till the party of the century . . .!

More chanting. Music fades . . .

In the sports hall, **Kemi** *is lying on the floor, groaning.*

Norah *stands over* **Kemi** *triumphantly. She slams the mat three times.* **Kemi** *stops groaning abruptly.*

Kemi   I'd call that my personal best.

Norah   But in the Atomic Drop, you need to run at me faster, like Lily said. Then I can fling you even further.

Kemi   Ok, ok, I'll try.

Lily *runs in, breathless.*

Lily   We have a problem! We're not allowed to wrestle!

Norah   What?!

Lily   It's boys only. Girls aren't allowed in the ring. We get a hair-braiding table.

Norah   I beg your pardon?

Lily   A hair-braiding table.

Kemi   I can braid my hair in my own time, thank you. I want to wrestle!

Norah   But – what?! Loads of girls have been invited.

Lily   They're supposed to stay on the patio and cheer for the boys.

Norah   What about the girls in WWE? Chyna and Trish Stratus?

Lily   They're grown women. We're just kids. We don't have a choice.

Norah   But we've worked so hard! Kemi's perfected her losing groan.

(*To* **Kemi**.) Show her.

Kemi *groans at* **Lily**.

Norah   See? We're ready!

Lily   They won't let you in the ring! You're girls! And – let's be real – but everyone knows you're dweebs.

Kemi   For now. But tomorrow, we close the door on our dweeby pasts. Tomorrow we transform –

Norah   Regenerate –

Kemi   And we become . . . we become . . . .

Lily   You don't even have wrestler names!

Norah We will!

Kemi We so will!

Norah We have to do this, we have to wrestle.

Lily You can't. Sorry. Bentley makes the rules.

He said.

Kemi Plead your case. Ask him to reconsider –

Norah Tell him his rules are outdated and nonsensical!

Lily I can't! No one listens to me.

Pause.

I'm sorry.

Pause.

I guess I'll do a smaller experiment. Magnets . . .

Norah *and* **Kemi** *are gutted.*

Kemi MASKS! Wrestling masks! We'll cover our faces, sneak into the garden, unleash ourselves into the ring, smash through our routine –

Norah And when the bell rings and the crowd chants our names, we'll rip off our disguises and reveal our true identities!

Kemi And by then, nobody will care that we're girls because they'll be awestuck by our SPORTING PROWESS!

Please, Lily.

Norah Don't you want to break the rules, just this once?

Pause.

Lily Your wrestler names better be awesome.

They do a high ten.

Eight

Afternoon break.

Plastic cups, elastic bands, printed diagrams and science equipment galore. In the corner, the plastic bins are piled up under a huge black sheet.

Norah, **Kemi** *and* **Lily** *are in lab coats and safety goggles.*

Norah A vortex is a spinning flow of fluid or gas.

Kemi Air is made up of teeny tiny particles – bits of nitrogen and oxygen, and water, and some other stuff. They're so small you can't see them.

She picks up a plastic cup. There's a hole cut in the bottom, and a small plastic sheet and an elasticated band attached to the wider end. It's a mini DIY air cannon.

Norah So when you ping the diaphragm – this bit – it hits a load of air particles. They fly forwards and hit the particles in front of them –

Kemi And they hit the particles in front of them, and so on. It's a chain reaction.

Lily Chain reaction. Cool.

Kemi It starts with the rubber band, and becomes more powerful when it reaches the hole here –

She points to the narrow end of the cup, which has a hole cut in it.

Norah Because the hole is smaller. So the air particles in the hole push forwards at a higher speed.

Kemi The air in the middle moves faster than the air at the edge, so it spins into a doughnut shape.

She fires the mini air cannon at **Lily**'s *face. She's hit with a tiny puff of air.*

Lily So it's like a slingshot, but for air?

Kemi Exactly.

Lily That is pretty cool.

Norah It's easier to see the doughnut shape if the cup is full of smoke or mist. The same rules apply for larger air cannons.

Kemi We got you three.

Norah To make your experiment as impactful as possible.

Kemi We've written it all down, so you can explain it to the class. We've printed thirty handouts with diagrams and links.

Lily Whoa.

They give **Lily** *the handouts.*

Norah Don't be scared. You've coached two pro wrestlers – a science experiment will be a walk in the park.

Lily *smiles.*

Lily Got something for you. For tomorrow.

She pulls two costumes out of her bag.

Sparkly one. And I think this one's a swimming costume.

She passes one to each of them. **Norah** *and* **Kemi** *hold them up.*

Kemi Whoa!

Kemi's *is a sparkly gymnastics bodysuit, and* **Norah**'s *is an iridescent, mermaid-scaled swimming costume.*

Norah Where did you get these?!

Lily My auntie works at the charity shop.

Kemi Nice . . .

Lily And these –

She hands over two wrestling masks. They immediately put them on.

Kemi They're proper – proper wrestling masks!

Lily   I told my dad they were for Bentley. Is that bad?

Kemi   It's genius!

Norah   We look like real wrestlers.

Kemi   We're going to smash it right out of the ring!

Norah   Hundy-p. We'll be dweebs no more –

Kemi   We'll be pro wrestlers!

The door flies open and **Bentley** *storms in.*

Kemi *and* **Norah** *throw themselves behind the pile of plastic bins.*

Bentley *sees* **Lily** *in her lab coat and goggles.*

Bentley   What are you doing?

Lily   Working on my science experiment. Alone. On my own.

Bentley   You look like a total dweeb.

Lily *takes the goggles off.*

Lily   What d'you – what are you doing in here?

Pause.

Bentley   Is everything ready for the hair-braiding table, cos it better be ready, yeah?! IS IT READY?

Lily   Yes.

Bentley   Ok. Good. Sick. Laters.

He punches the air and goes.

Kemi *and* **Norah** *emerge from their hiding place, jaws dropped in pure terror.*

Lily   He's gone.

Kemi   Oh. My. Days.

Norah   Do you think he saw anything? Do you think he could smell us?! He sniffed. I saw him sniffing.

Lily That was so weird.

Norah He's onto us! He knows. It's over! This whole elaborate plan is coming crumbling down!

Kemi Norah.

Norah Our attempts are for nothing. Our efforts are meaningless!

Kemi Norah! Where is the sign?

Norah What?

Kemi For the 'Extremely Serious Homework Club'?

Pause.

Norah Oh no! I forgot. I'm so sorry, I totally forgot!

Kemi You can't drop the ball like that! You nearly destroyed our whole plan!

Norah It was a mistake! I haven't slept for five days, this schedule is gruelling!

Kemi How can I trust you to fling me through the air if you can't even remember to put up the sign?!

Norah I'm your co-wrestler! You can trust me.

Kemi Can I?!

Norah Of course you can. I'm your best friend.

Kemi Used to be. Used to be.

A stand-off. Then –

Lily What d'you mean 'used to be'?!

Norah Kemi, please –

Kemi Norah stole my ancient Egyptians project. She wrote her name on the top and handed it in, and Mrs Gaskin gave her one hundred per cent.

Norah Kemi!

Kemi And she put my name on her project, and I got my lowest grade of ALL TIME.

Norah You got eighty-seven per cent. That's still good.

Kemi I deserved a hundred per cent. My project was perfect, I wrote it in hieroglyphics!

Norah Because your mum took you to the British Museum every single day of half-term. Nobody taught me hieroglyphics.

Kemi That doesn't make it ok to cheat! We were best friends, and you betrayed me.

Norah I think you're over-reacting.

Kemi Me?

Norah Yeah!

Kemi And I know what you're like. When we're wrestling champions, you'll go around telling everyone it was your idea. But it wasn't. It was mine!

Norah It's not that big a deal.

Kemi You're so scared of coming second that you stole my actual work!

Norah Your work was only good because your mum helped you. You had help, I never have help!

Kemi I'm smarter than you! Get over it.

Norah You really think you can make yourself cool by pretending to be a wrestler? You can't! No matter what you do, within one millisecond of you starting at Harris Academy, the whole school will know what you are – boring, studious and socially inept! Bentley's right. You are a dweeb. A complete and utter DWEEB!

Silence . . .

Kemi *goes to the door.*

Lily Kemi?

Kemi (*to* **Norah**)   I'll go to the party. I'll do the routine. But after that, you're on your own. Don't speak to me. Don't look at me.

(*To* **Lily**.) Take the experiment home. Norah can help you finish it. She's the best at science.

(*To* **Norah**.) Good luck at Harris Academy.

Kemi *leaves.*

Norah *is stunned.* **Lily** *doesn't know what to say.* **Norah** *and* **Lily** *tidy up in silence.*

Nine A

Lily *closes her bedroom door.*

She looks at all of the equipment for her experiment. She opens the handout and begins to study.

Nine B

Later that evening. Night falls. Music plays. **Kemi** *closes her bedroom door.*

She takes the sparkly bodysuit out of her pocket and looks at it.

Nine C

Norah *closes her bedroom door.*

She pulls out the mermaid swimming costume.

Nine D

Bentley's *bedroom.*

He drapes a large piece of sparkly fabric over his shoulders like a cape.

He swishes it in the mirror and admires himself.

He adds the champion's belt. He takes a deep breath.

Ten

Lily *and* **Bentley**'s *front drive. A large front door with impressive bin storage to one side.*

Behind the house, **Bentley**'s *party is in full swing. Wrestling music blasts, interrupted by the occasional ring of a bell and the cheer of thirty eleven-year-olds.*

Norah *approaches the front door wearing her wrestling outfit and carrying her mask.*

She waits, nervously, until . . .

Kemi *approaches, also in her wrestling outfit.*

They stand, separately, in silence. Until . . .

Lily (*now with multiple hair-braids*) *appears in the doorway.*

Lily The grown-ups have gone to Sainsbury's to get more drinks.

Norah All of them?

Lily Yep.

Norah That's so irresponsible!

Lily Bentley's in charge. He's downed a full-sized bottle of Coke. He's absolutely buzzing. He's flipped the hair-braiding table into next door's garden!

Lily We have to stick to our plan like glue. And remember, if anyone asks, you're –

Norah Brad.

Kemi Jason.

They put their masks on.

Norah Let's recap – when Bentley opens the buffet, we pounce.

Lily It's really happening. We're breaking the rules. We're breaking the rules!

Kemi Wait! Coach, I need to tell you something. Confidentially.

Norah If you have something to say, you can share it with the group.

Kemi Fine.

Pause.

I faint at the sight of blood.

Lily . . . What!?

Kemi It's a psychological malfunction. I pass out. Completely. One drop and I'm a goner. It's called vasovagal syncope.

Norah Why didn't you tell us before?

Kemi Excuse me, please. This is a matter for my coach to resolve.

Lily Swap roles.

Kemi What!?

Lily (*to* **Kemi**) If you become the Face, you'll do more of the lifting. There's less chance of you being injured.

Norah But I'm the Face. I'm supposed to win.

Lily Nobody wins if Kemi passes out.

Bentley *bursts out of the front door, holding a rotisserie chicken and jittering under the influence of a huge amount of sugar.*

Bentley THE BUFFET IS OPEN!

They freeze. **Bentley** *sees them.*

All right, lads. You look sick. Wooooo!

He goes.

Kemi I agree with Lily. We have to swap roles.

Norah But I won the thumb war! I deserve to be the Face!

Kemi And I deserve to stay conscious!

Norah Kemi!

Kemi You don't always have to win!

Norah Oh, here we go again!

Lily People! Listen to your coach!

*They are all startled by **Lily**'s newfound leadership skills.*

Swap roles or it's over.

A standoff.

Norah Fine. I'll do it. I'll take one for the team. I'll be the Heel.

Lily Good. Here's the plan:

Kemi – you start with the DDT. Norah comes back with the X Chromosome. Got it? Got it?!

They both nod.

Kemi does the rope jump followed by the Big Boot, and then the People's Elbow. Norah returns with the Stone Cold Stunner. You work the crowd. You rile them up. You get them chanting your names. They cheer. They boo. And then, silence falls, and Norah – you run at Kemi, she flings you through the air and slams you to the mat – the Atomic Drop. The crowd goes wild, and Kemi is crowned the winner. Job done. Ok?

Kemi/Norah Yes, coach.

Lily It's now or never. Let's do this.

Eleven

The garden. Music plays. A mountain of rotisserie chickens are piled up on a buffet table. There are banners reading 'Bentley's Year 6 Leavers' Party', along with WWE balloons. Brock Lesnar's face is printed on paper plates, and a sprinkling of beads and ribbons are scattered where the hair-braiding table used to be.

Dominating the garden is an enormous wrestling ring, complete with ropes, pillars and a crash mat.

Lily, *unnoticed, drags the wheelie bins into the garden.* **Bentley** *puts down the loudhailer.*

Bentley   Lily – get me a chicken! Where's my sister?! LILY?!

Lily *grabs the microphone and adopts her own announcer voice.*

Lily   It's time! Cover your ears, and brace for high velocity, it's everybody's hero and the Face you've been waiting for. Give up for . . .

A boom! The crowd cheers as **Kemi** *emerges dressed in the sparkly bodysuit and wrestling mask.*

Kemi   The Sonic Boom!

She runs into the ring, gets the audience to chant her name and punches the air as her entrance music plays . . .

And in opposition . . . serving intergalactic realness – the baddie of your nightmares, the Heel to end all Heels . . .

Lily *leads the crowd to boo as* **Norah** *pops open the wheelie bin and clambers out, wearing the mermaid swimming costume and wrestling mask. She looks the business.*

Norah   Quantum Dread!

She joins **Kemi** *in the ring, as – together with* **Lily** *– they encourage boos and jeers from the audience.*

Bentley *watches while chomping on a chicken drumstick.*

Norah *and* **Kemi** *face each other.*

Arena lights spin, music fades and everything focuses in on **Norah** *and* **Kemi**.

Lily (*into the loudhailer*) It's showtime . . . .

Kemi *grabs* **Norah** *in a headlock and drops to the mat, driving* **Norah**'s *head to the ground.*

Lily It's a DDT from The Sonic Boom . . . but Quantum Dread breaks free!

Norah *jumps up and grabs* **Kemi**.

Lily And Quantum Dread responds with – yes it is – it's the X Chromosome.

Lily *smacks the mat.*

One – two –

The crowd goes wild!

Kemi *jumps up from the floor.*

No-ones going down without a fight . . .

Norah *scrapes the floor with her foot, like a matador.*

But The Sonic Boom strikes back with The Big Boot!

Kemi *reveals her elbow and shows it to the crowd.*

It's pointy. It's sharp. There's nothing funny about this bone-

Kemi *runs the ropes, bounces off them, jumps over*

Norah *and drops an elbow to her chest!*

The People's Elbow!

The crowd oohs and aahs.

These two mystery wrestlers are at the top of their game. It couldn't be a closer match.

Norah *grabs* **Kemi**'s *head in a face-lock with one arm, then drops to a seated position, forcing* **Kemi**'s *head to meet her shoulder.*

Lily Quantum Dread delivers a Stone Cold Stunner, and Kemi – sorry – The Sonic Boom – is down!

Groans and cheers from the crowd. **Norah** *and* **Kemi** *jump up and bounce around the ring, fake jeering at each other and encouraging cheers from the crowd.*

Lily The Sonic Boom is not going to take this lying down.

Slow motion and epic music as **Kemi** *lifts* **Norah** *and they embark on . . .*

The Atomic Drop!

They execute it perfectly. **Norah** *hits the mat,* **Kemi** *pins her,* **Lily** *runs into position beside them and smacks the mat –*

One – two – three!

A bell rings out.

We have a champion!

Lily *raises* **Kemi**'s *hand and* **Kemi** *runs around the ring as* **Norah** *groans dramatically on the floor.*

Lily But a seriously awesome effort from Quantum Dread.

Kemi *helps* **Norah** *up.*

Norah *and* **Kemi** *strut around the ring as the crowd goes wild!*

They rip their masks off. Lights snap up. Music cuts. Silence.

Kemi It's us! Me and Norah!

Norah Also known as Quantum Dread and The Sonic Boom!

Bentley You weren't invited. You're dweebs.

Kemi Not any more. We're pro wrestlers now.

Bentley You two are DWEEBS!

Norah No, Bentley –

Kemi We used to be dweebs, but now we're heroes!

Norah Now we're wrestlers!

Bentley You want to wrestle? That's cool. You can wrestle ME!

Bentley's *music starts. It's threatening, ominous.*

Bentley I'm gonna slam you!

Kemi What?!

Bentley Destroy you! Sis! Prepare my entrance!

Bentley *leaves to get ready to make his entrance.*

Kemi *and* **Norah** *look at* **Lily**. *She hesitates, then runs off. Hope hangs by a thread.*

Norah Kemi, I need to say something. In case – in case I don't make it. I'm sorry I stole your ancient Egyptians project. It was extremely bad form. If I survive, I promise I'll confess to Mrs Gaskin.

Kemi Apology accepted. I didn't really go to Space Camp. I lied. I wanted to make you jealous.

Norah Kemi!

Kemi I miss when we had sleepovers.

Norah Me too.

Kemi If, by some miracle, we live, you could maybe – maybe come to mine next weekend?

Bentley's *entrance music plays and he struts into the ring, being 'The Bentley'.*

Bentley Let's go! Who am I fighting first? Sparkly dweeb or rainbow dweeb?

Kemi Both of us.

Norah Yeah! Both of us!

Bentley Two on one? Not a problem for The Bentley!

Kemi *and* **Norah** *enter the ring.*

A bit of posturing and circling. Then, **Bentley** *approaches* **Kemi**. *He backs her into a corner. He raises his fist.*

Bentley Prepare to bleed!

Kemi Spare me!

Norah *steps in front of* **Kemi**.

Norah Fight me – fight me first.

Bentley You're going DOWN!

Norah *and* **Kemi** *cower.* **Bentley** *raises his fist to pulverize* **Norah** *when a voice rings out –*

Everyone turns to see . . .

An enormous, Batmobile-looking death-vehicle made of six huge plastic bins riding out onto the lawn!

At the wheel is **Lily**, *lab coat and safety goggles on, wind in her hair, yelling into the loudhailer. She looks like a modern-day, ten-year-old Boudicca.*

Metallica plays as the headlights beam and built-in lasers swing around to track **Bentley**.

Bentley Sis?

Lily It's Lily! Hands up. Surrender.

Bentley Or what?

Lily Or I'll destroy you with the power of nerd! Chain reaction!

She fires the top air cannon and a ring of green smoke launches slowly across the garden towards **Bentley**.

Bentley Is that all you've got? A smokey doughnut?

Lily That's just the starter.

She grabs a rotisserie chicken and stuffs it into the front of one of the air cannons.

Eat chicken, Bentley!

*She fires the chicken at **Bentley**!*

*Absolute chaos breaks out. **Norah** and **Kemi** scramble out of the ring and form a conveyor belt to help **Lily** reload the air cannons.*

*Forty rotisserie chickens are fired across the wrestling ring (and over the audience). But **Bentley** dodges them all.*

He fights back – flinging paper plates like frisbees. It's carnage.

Finally, he is backed into the corner of the wrestling ring.

Kemi (*to* **Lily**) Two chickens left!

Norah *passes a chicken to* **Kemi**, *who throws it to* **Lily**.

Norah I'll take him down!

Lily *fires the chicken. It flies across the ring – and hits* **Kemi** *square in the face.*

Silence.

The chicken falls to the floor. **Kemi** *clutches her nose. Everything happens in slow-mo.*

Kemi I'm bleeding.

Norah It's only a little bit, it's not much at all –

Kemi Must – not – faint! It's – the – final – chicken!

Epic music as she staggers across the ring, carrying the final chicken towards **Lily**. *She makes it to the air cannon pyramid.*

Lily *loads the final chicken into the air cannon. She closes in on* **Bentley**. *They've got him cornered.*

Normal speed resumes as **Lily** *closes in on* **Bentley** *– she's at close range. They've got him now!*

Kemi Hit him with the chicken!

Lily 'Can you smell what the coach is cooking?!'

She's about to fire it right at him –

Bentley Stop! It's not my fault! I hate this, I hate it – I – I didn't even want a wrestling party!

It was Dad's idea.

Lily (*to* **Norah** *and* **Kemi**) He's lying. He just doesn't want to get hit with a chicken.

Bentley I'm not lying! Dad said if I show everyone how strong I am, I'll be ok in Year 7. But – but I don't even like wrestling.

Lily Then why are you always watching it?

Silence.

See? You're a liar.

She prepares to fire the chicken. There's no escape for **Bentley**.

Bentley I like the costumes. The mask, the capes . . . the boots.

I like sewing. I sewed it by hand.

Pause.

I found a sewing box in the Sports Hall. It's under my bed.

Three thousand sequins. Yep. There. I said it. Now you can all laugh at me.

Nobody laughs.

Norah You made your own wrestling costume?!

Kemi Impeccable detailing.

Bentley It's a custom spandex unitard inspired by the art and culture of the Luchadores. I wouldn't make that up. The wrestling's Dad's thing. Not mine.

Pause.

I – don't tell him. Please.

Pause.

Lily On one condition. I want a new rule. Girls can wrestle.

Bentley Ok, ok, girls can wrestle.

Lily And you're gonna make me an awesome costume. Deal?

Bentley Deal! Sequins, feathers, embroidered shoulder-pads! I'll sketch some designs this evening.

Norah Bentley – this is mega dweeby.

Bentley I know.

Norah Mega dweeby. And mega cool.

Bentley Both?

Pause.

Kemi Can something be dweeby *and* cool?

Norah An exciting hypothesis. Let's test it.

Kemi Example: writing a homework project in fluent hieroglyphics. So dweeby.

Norah And so cool. Example: Creating a ninety-minute presentation on French Cave paintings and Modern Japanese wrestling. Dweeby.

Kemi And yet so cool.

Lily Example: Using Newton's three laws of motion to fire forty-two rotisserie chickens across your garden at your big brother.

Norah Pure dweeb!

Bentley And quite cool, to be fair.

Norah Scientists, wrestlers, artistes – I believe we have proved that dweebiness is cool.

Bentley Sick.

Norah/Kemi Hundy-p.

Bentley Hundy-what?

Lily Hands in.

She and **Bentley** *put their hands in the middle.* **Norah** *and* **Kemi** *don't know what to do.*

Lily You put your hands on top. It's a team thing.

They do it.

Go, team – wait – what's our team name?

Norah Wrestling-dweebs?

Bentley W-W-Dweeb?

Kemi Dweeb-mania – like Wrestle Mania?

Norah Dweeb-A-Mania?

Kemi Yes! Dweeb-A-Mania.

Lily One – two – three –

All DWEEB-A-MANIA!

End.

www.ingramcontent.com/pod-product-compliance
Lightning Source LLC
Chambersburg PA
CBHW040323050426
42453CB00018B/2444